What do we think about

Drugs?

Karen Bryant-Mole

HODDER
Wayland

an imprint of Hodder Children's Books

Titles in the series

What do we think about ...

Adoption • Alcohol • Bullying
Death • Disability • Drugs
Family Break-Up • Our Environment

All Hodder Wayland books encourage children to read and help them improve their literacy.

✓ The contents page, page numbers, headings and index help locate specific pieces of information.

✓ The glossary reinforces alphabetic knowledge and extends vocabulary.

✓ The further information section suggests other books dealing with the same subject.

✓ Find out more about how this book is specifically relevant to the National Literacy Strategy on page 31.

Editor: Elizabeth Gogerly
Consultant: John Bennett, a Health Education Coordinator
Cover designer: Jan Sterling
Designer: Jean Wheeler
Photo stylist: Gina Brown
Production controller: Carol Titchener

First published in Great Britain 1999 by Wayland (Publishers) Limited.
This edition published in 2001 by Hodder Wayland, an imprint of Hodder Children's Books
© Hodder Wayland 1999

British Library Cataloguing in Publication Data
Bryant-Mole, Karen
What do we think about drugs?
1. Drug abuse – Juvenile literature 2. Drugs of abuse – Juvenile literature
I. Title II. Drugs
362.2'9

ISBN 07502 3402 4

Printed and bound in Grafiasa, Porto, Portugal

Picture acknowledgements
Family Life Pictures/ Angela Hampton 5, 11, 12, 15, 17, 24, 26; David Hoffman 20; Eye Ubiquitous cover (background); Format/ Joanne O'Brien 22; Martyn F. Chillmaid cover (main), 9, 6,18, 19, 21, 23; Photofusion/ Mark Campbell 13; Sally and Richard Greenhill 7; Skjold Photographs 8, 27; Tony Stone 4, 6, 10, 14, 25.
Many thanks to the pupils of Birchensale Middle School in Redditch who acted as models for some of the photographs in this book.

Contents

What are drugs?

One good way of understanding what drugs are, is to compare them to food.

You eat food every day. Food is taken into your body and used by your body to keep itself going.

Drugs are also things that are taken into the body. But, instead of feeding the body, drugs make changes to it.

Medicines

Some drugs are helpful. The changes they make to the body can stop people from getting diseases or make them better if they do become ill.

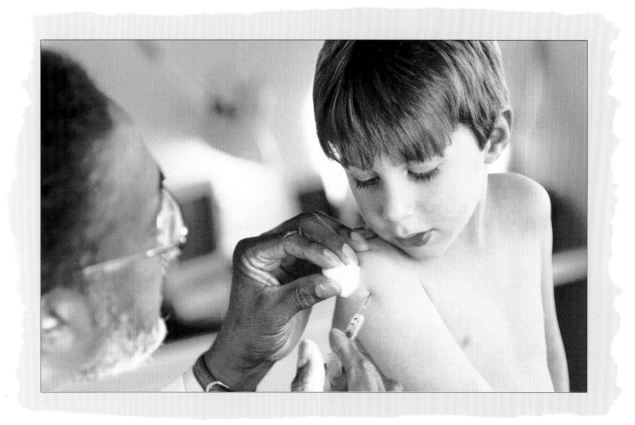

Drugs like these are called medicines. They can be given to you in different ways, such as in a pill or an injection.

All drugs, including medicines, can be dangerous.

It is important to take the correct amount and no more.

Illegal drugs

Medicines can be given to people by doctors, nurses and dentists.

Some medicines can be bought at chemists. People are allowed to have drugs like these.

There are other drugs, though, that people are not allowed to have or to sell.

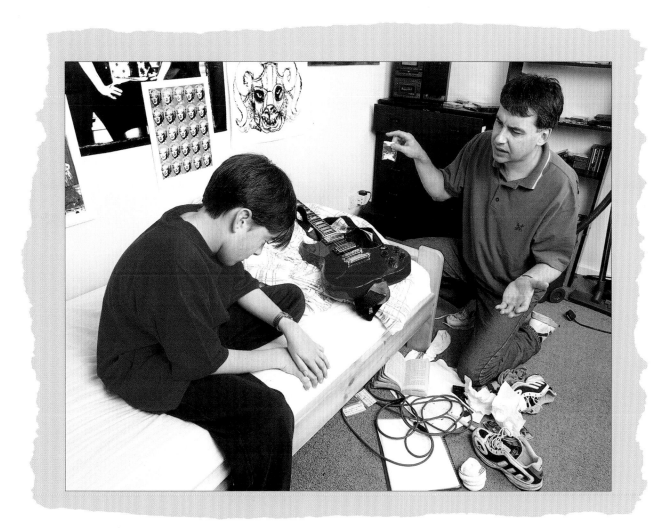

These drugs are called illegal drugs.
Illegal means 'against the law'.

What are drugs called?

There are many different types of illegal drug. They are taken into the body in different ways. Some are swallowed, some are smoked, some are injected.

Illegal drugs have proper names, such as heroin and cocaine. They also have nicknames, such as snow, brown and smack.

When people first take illegal drugs, it is not because they need to take them but because they want to take them.

Changes

Different drugs make different sorts of changes to a person's body. Some make the person feel relaxed.

Others make the person feel full of energy. But these changes can also damage people's bodies, especially if the drugs are taken often.

Some drugs are addictive. This means that the body starts to need that drug. It is very difficult to stop taking a drug if the body is addicted to it.

Control

Unless you are ill, or want to prevent an illness, you do not need drugs of any sort.

Your body works perfectly, just as it is. And you are completely in control of your own body.

People who take drugs are not in control of their bodies.

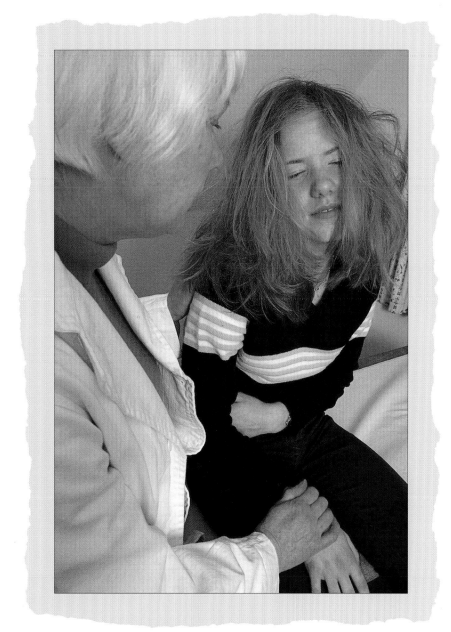

They are putting something into their bodies that will make changes that they cannot control.

Why do people take drugs?

Even though drugs can be bad for people, some people still choose to take them.

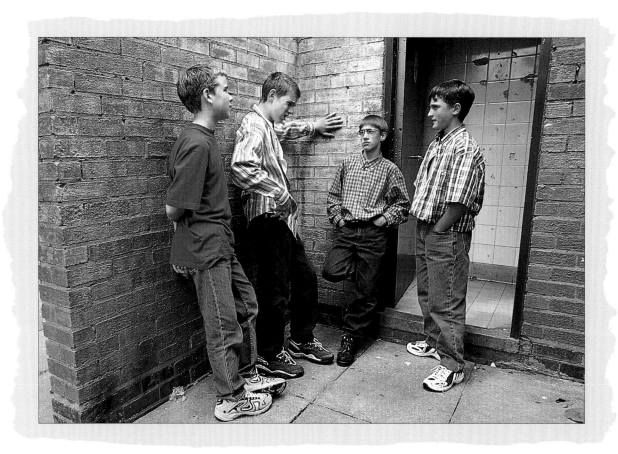

Some people do not know what drugs can do to them. Other people know what they can do but do not care because they like the effects that the drugs have.

Often, young people like to do the same things as their friends. People sometimes take drugs just because their friends take them.

Saying 'no'

Tom had two friends, who said that they were going to try some drugs. They told Tom that unless he tried them too they wouldn't be his friend any more.

Tom thought about it and decided that he didn't want to try drugs. He decided he would find new friends who liked doing the same things as him.

Saying 'no' to drugs can be difficult. But it's your body. You decide what goes into it. Don't be bullied into doing something you don't want to do.

Why 'no' is a good choice

Deciding to say 'no' to drugs is a good choice to make. There are many people who now take drugs who wish that they had said 'no'.

Drugs are expensive. Melanie spent all her money on drugs and couldn't pay the rent on her flat. Now she is homeless.

The police had arrested Mark a number of times for having illegal drugs. Eventually he was sent to prison. Mark has been released but he can't get a job.

Who sells drugs?

People who sell drugs are called drug dealers. Being a drug dealer is illegal.

Drug dealers can be put in prison for many years. They take the risk of getting caught because they want the money.

Simon had become addicted to drugs but couldn't afford to buy them. He started to sell drugs to his friends to get money for his own drugs.

He didn't care that he could be ruining their lives as well as his own.

Helping

People who take drugs might find it difficult to give them up but it is not impossible.

There are helplines that people can ring to get advice. People can talk to other people who understand their problems.

There are clinics, where the doctors and nurses are trained to help people give up drugs.

The most important thing is that the person who takes the drugs actually wants to give up.

Choices

At the moment, your parents probably make most of the choices in your life, such as where you live and what time you go to bed. Part of growing up is about learning to make your own choices.

You will be able to choose your own way of life. It could be a life that is controlled by expensive drugs which could affect your health and lead to you being put in prison.

Or it could be a happy, fun life that you control, with the freedom to spend the money you earn on whatever you want.

Which life will you choose?

Notes for parents and teachers

This book is designed to help young children understand what drugs are, to teach them the difference between legal and illegal drugs and to make them aware of some of the dangers and consequences of taking illegal drugs.

You could also use this book to help children appreciate the importance of looking after their bodies in other ways, for example, having a healthy diet and an active lifestyle. You could discuss the role of medicine with children, stressing the importance of taking the correct dose and never taking medicines that have been prescribed to someone else. Children could also be encouraged to think about all the things they enjoy about life and to recognize that no one really needs to take drugs to have a good time.

However, it is a fact of life that drugs are part of our society. Sooner or later, the child or children in your care will come across them. Children cannot make choices without information. This book gives children basic, but accurate, information about drugs. Sometimes, adults choose not to talk to children about drugs, in the belief that in so doing they are shielding them from harm. It often has the opposite effect. If children do not know of the risks and consequences involved, they can see no reason why they should not experiment with drugs.

Knowledge puts your child in a position of strength and allows him or her to understand the importance of making the right decision. It is also important for you, as parents and teachers, to be aware of the facts about drugs, so that you can give children accurate answers to their questions.

There are very many reasons why young people turn to drugs. They include boredom, a means of escaping problems, a desire to rebel and pressure from their friends. You can never guarantee that someone will not try taking drugs. What you can do, however, is give them the best possible means to make the decision that drugs are not for them. The way to do this is through education and information.

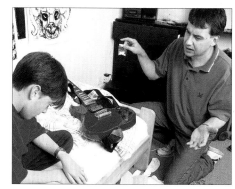

Glossary

clinic Where people can go to see a doctor or nurse.

compare Look at two things and see how they are the same and how they are different.

damage Cause harm.

diseases Particular types of illnesses.

injected Squirt through the skin, into the body, using a needle and a tube called a syringe.

prevent Stop something happening.

relaxed Feel very calm, without any worries.

rent Money that is paid to the person who owns the building.

Further information

Organizations which provide information for parents, teachers and children about drugs include:

Health Education Authority
Trevelyan House
30 Great Peter Street
London SWIP 2HW
Tel: 0171 222 5300

ISDD (the Institute for the
   Study of Drug Dependence)
Waterbridge House
32-36 Loman Street
London SE1 OEE
Tel: 0171 928 1211

Central Drugs Prevention Unit
Home Office
Room 354
Horseferry House
Dean Ryle Street
London SW1P 2AW
Tel: 0171 217 8631

The Scottish Drugs Forum
5th Floor Shaftesbury House
5 Waterloo Street
Glasgow G2 6AY
Tel: 0141 221 1175

The Welsh Office
Cathays Park
Cardiff CF1 3NQ
Tel: 01222 825 592

Health Promotion Branch
DHSS Upper Newtownards Road
Belfast BT4 3SF
Tel: 01232 524 234

Organizations which support drug users and their families include:

National Drugs Helpline
Tel: 0800 776 600

ADFAM (the national helpline for
   family and friends of drug users)
Waterbridge House
32-36 Loman Street
London SE1 OEE
Tel: 0171 928 8900

Release 'Drugs in School Helpline'
Tel: 0345 366 666

Books to read

For older readers:

Dealing with Substance Abuse by Yvette Solomon and John Coleman (Wayland, 1995)

Face the Facts: Drugs by Adrian King (Wayland, 1997)

We're Talking About Drugs by Jenny Bryan (Wayland, 1995)

What Do You Know About Drugs by Pete Sanders and Steve Myers (Watts, 1995)

For parents and teachers:

A Parents' Guide to Drugs and Solvents (get a free copy by ringing the National Drugs Helpline)

Drug Abuse Briefing (ISDD, teacher's edition, 1996)

Drugs Issues for Schools by Colin Chapman (ISDD)

Street Drugs by Andrew Tyler (New English Library)

Use this book for teaching literacy

This book can help you in the literacy hour in the following ways:

✔ Children can discuss themes and link them to their own experiences.

✔ They can discuss the case studies and think about how they might behave in similar situations

✔ They can compare this book with fictional stories about drugs to show how similar information can be presented in different ways.

✔ They can try rewriting some of the situations described in the form of a story.

Index